·Cooking for Today·

COOKING ON A BUDGET

·*Cooking for Today*·

COOKING ON A BUDGET

SUE ASHWORTH

·PARRAGON·

First published in Great Britain in 1996 by
Parragon Book Service Ltd
Unit 13–17
Avonbridge Trading Estate
Atlantic Road
Avonmouth
Bristol BS11 9QD

ISBN 0-7525-1802-X

Produced by Haldane Mason, London

Printed in Italy

Acknowledgements:
Art Direction: Ron Samuels
Editor: Vicky Hanson
Series Design: Pedro & Frances Prá-Lopez/Kingfisher Design, London
Page Design: Somewhere Creative
Photography & Styling: Amanda Heywood
Home Economist: Sue Ashworth
Assistant Home Economist: Yvonne Melville

Photographs on pages 6, 20, 34, 48 & 62 reproduced by permission of
ZEFA Picture Library (UK) Ltd.

Note:
Cup measurements in this book are for American cups. Tablespoons are assumed to be 15 ml.
Unless otherwise stated, milk is assumed to be full-fat, eggs are standard size 2 and
pepper is freshly ground black pepper.

Contents

❧

SOUPS & STEWS *page* 7

Cream Cheese & Fresh Herb Soup 8
Lentil & Parsnip Pottage 10
Lamb & Barley Broth 12
Italian Fish Stew 15
Chicken & Chilli Bean Pot 16
Beef Goulash 18

PIES & BAKES *page* 21

Baked Stuffed Onions 22
Winter Vegetable Cobbler 24
Mariner's Pie 26
Minced (Ground) Lamb & Potato Moussaka 29
Savoury Batter Puddings with Thyme & Onion
    Sauce 30
Bacon, Onion & Potato Hotpot 32

PASTA, RICE & GRAINS *page* 35

Thai-Style Chicken Fried Rice 36
Mushroom & Parmesan Risotto 38
Pasta with Pine Nuts (Kernels) & Blue Cheese 41
Smoked Fish Lasagne 42
Quick Chinese Chicken with Noodles 44
Moroccan Vegetable Couscous 46

EGGS & CHEESE *page* 49

Egg & Chick-Pea (Garbanzo Bean) Curry 50
Savoury Bread & Butter Pudding 52
Spinach & Cheese Pancake Stack 55
Chicken & Sweetcorn Puff 56
Golden Cheese & Leek Potato Cakes 58
Flamenco Eggs 60

DESSERTS *page* 63

Chocolate Bread Pudding 64
Quick Syrup Sponge 66
Pancakes with Apples & Butterscotch Sauce 68
Apricot & Banana Queen of Puddings 70
Baked Semolina Pudding with Spiced Plums 73
Coffee Cream Trifle 74

KEEPING TO A BUDGET *page* 76

Index 80

CHAPTER ONE

Soups & Stews

Tasty, filling and nutritious, soups and stews are the original comfort food. Perfect for when you are feeling cold and hungry, these recipes will satisfy your appetite and fill you to the brim – even when you're having to feed everyone on a budget.

The trick is to make the most of fresh seasonal vegetables, and to treat them with flair and a pinch of imagination. Some of the cheapest ingredients are transformed into something special in the recipes in this chapter. Who would have thought that a few handfuls of fresh herbs from the garden could be transformed into the most delicious summer soup (see page 8)? And who wouldn't enjoy the aromas from the slow-cooked Lamb and Barley Broth (see page 12) as it bubbles away on the stove?

So try these ideas and introduce some superb new recipes into your repertoire – you'll be delighted with the results. What's more, you'll find that your purse strings won't be overstretched.

Opposite: *Use ingredients that are in season and you'll find that soups and stews are so economical.*

STEP 1

STEP 2

STEP 3

STEP 4

CREAM CHEESE & FRESH HERB SOUP

Make the most of home-grown herbs to create this wonderfully creamy soup with its marvellous garden-fresh fragrance.

SERVES 4

30 g/ 1 oz/ 2 tbsp butter or margarine
2 onions, chopped
900 ml/ 1¹/₂ pints/ 3¹/₂ cups vegetable stock
30 g/ 1 oz coarsely chopped mixed fresh
  herbs, such as parsley, chives, thyme,
  basil and oregano
200 g/ 7 oz/ 1 cup full-fat soft cheese
1 tbsp cornflour (cornstarch)
1 tbsp milk
chopped fresh chives to garnish

1 Melt the butter or margarine in a large saucepan and add the onions. Fry for 2 minutes, then cover and turn the heat to low. Allow the onions to cook gently for 5 minutes, then remove the lid.

2 Add the stock and herbs to the saucepan. Bring to the boil, then turn down the heat. Cover and simmer gently for 20 minutes.

3 Remove the saucepan from the heat. Blend the soup with a hand blender or in a food processor or blender for about 15 seconds, until smooth. Alternatively, press it through a sieve (strainer). Return the soup to the saucepan.

4 Reserve a little of the cheese for garnish. Spoon the remaining cheese into the soup and whisk until the cheese is incorporated.

5 Mix the cornflour (cornstarch) with the milk, then stir into the soup and heat, stirring constantly, until thickened and smooth.

6 Pour the soup into 4 warmed bowls. Spoon some of the reserved cheese into each bowl and garnish with chives. Serve at once.

SUMMER SOUP

In summer, this soup is wonderful when served chilled.

HERBS

Choose at least two different types of herb for this soup, and make sure that one of them is quite mild, so that the flavour is not overpowering.

STEP 1

STEP 2

STEP 3

STEP 4

LENTIL & PARSNIP POTTAGE

*Smooth and delicious, this soup has the most glorious golden colour
and fabulous flavour.*

Serves 4

3 slices streaky bacon, chopped
1 onion, chopped
2 carrots, chopped
2 parsnips, chopped
60 g/2 oz/⅓ cup red lentils
1 litre/1¾ pints/4 cups vegetable stock or
   water
salt and pepper
chopped fresh chives to garnish

1 Heat a large saucepan, add the
bacon and dry-fry for 5 minutes
until crisp and golden.

2 Add the onion, carrots and
parsnips and cook for about 5
minutes without browning.

3 Add the lentils to the saucepan and
stir to mix with the vegetables.

4 Add the stock to the saucepan and
bring to the boil. Cover and simmer
for 30–40 minutes until tender.

5 Transfer the soup to a blender or
food processor and blend for about
15 seconds until smooth. Alternatively,
press the soup through a sieve (strainer).

6 Return to the saucepan and reheat
gently until almost boiling. Season
to taste. Garnish with chives and serve.

VARIATIONS

Green or brown lentils can be used in
place of the red ones.

HAM

For a meatier soup which would make a
good main course, use a knuckle of ham in
place of the streaky bacon. Cook it for
1½–2 hours before adding the vegetables
and lentils and use the ham's cooking
liquid as the stock.

STEP 1

STEP 2

STEP 3

STEP 4

LAMB & BARLEY BROTH

Warming and nutritious, this broth is perfect for a cold winter's day. The slow cooking allows you to use one of the cheaper cuts of meat.

SERVES 4

1 tbsp vegetable oil
500 g/1 lb neck of lamb
1 large onion, sliced
2 carrots, sliced
2 leeks, sliced
1 litre/1 3/4 pints/4 cups vegetable stock
1 bay leaf
few sprigs of fresh parsley
60 g/2 oz/1/3 cup pearl barley

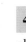 **1** Heat the oil in a large, heavy-based saucepan and add the pieces of lamb, turning them to seal and brown on both sides. Lift the lamb out of the pan and set aside.

2 Add the onion, carrots and leeks to the saucepan and cook gently for about 3 minutes.

3 Return the lamb to the saucepan and add the stock, bay leaf, parsley and pearl barley to the saucepan. Bring to the boil, then reduce the heat. Cover and simmer for 1½–2 hours until the lamb is tender.

4 Discard the parsley sprigs. Lift the pieces of lamb from the broth and allow them to cool slightly. Remove the bones and any fat and chop the meat. Return the lamb to the broth and reheat gently. Serve the broth in warmed serving bowls.

TIPS

This broth will taste even better if made the day before, as this allows the flavours to fully develop. It also means that any fat will solidify on the surface so you can then lift it off. Keep the broth in the refrigerator until required.

ONE-POT MEAL

If you like, make small dumplings and add them to the soup 20 minutes before serving for a more substantial meal.

ITALIAN FISH STEW

This wonderfully robust stew is full of fine Mediterranean flavours such as basil, lemon and tomato. As you can use any firm white fish, it's ideal for using whatever is the most economical.

STEP 1

SERVES 4

2 tbsp olive oil
2 red onions, finely chopped
1 garlic clove, crushed
2 courgettes (zucchini), sliced
425 g/14 oz can chopped tomatoes
900 ml/1½ pints/3½ cups fish or vegetable
    stock
90 g/3 oz dried pasta shapes
350 g/12 oz firm white fish, such as cod,
    haddock or hake
1 tbsp chopped fresh basil or oregano or
    1 tsp dried oregano
1 tsp grated lemon rind
1 tbsp cornflour (cornstarch)
1 tbsp water
salt and pepper
fresh basil or oregano sprigs to garnish

1 Heat the oil in a large saucepan and fry the onions and garlic for 5 minutes. Add the courgettes (zucchini) and cook for 2–3 minutes, stirring often.

2 Add the tomatoes and stock to the saucepan and bring to the boil. Add the pasta, cover and reduce the heat. Simmer for 5 minutes.

3 Skin and bone the fish, then cut it into chunks. Add to the saucepan

STEP 2

STEP 3

with the basil or oregano and lemon rind and cook gently for 5 minutes until the fish is opaque and flakes easily. Take care not to overcook it.

4 Blend the cornflour (cornstarch) with the water and stir into the stew. Cook gently for 2 minutes, stirring, until thickened. Season to taste and ladle into 4 warmed soup bowls. Garnish with basil or oregano sprigs and serve at once.

VARIATIONS

This recipe is a good way to use up a little leftover wine. Add a couple of tablespoons of dry white wine just before serving.

Canned chopped tomatoes can be bought with a variety of flavourings; those with herbs are perfect for this stew.

STEP 4

STEP 1

STEP 2

STEP 3

STEP 4

CHICKEN & CHILLI BEAN POT

This aromatic chicken dish has a spicy Mexican kick. Chicken thighs are not only more economical than breasts, they have much more flavour when cooked in this way.

SERVES 4

2 tbsp plain (all-purpose) flour
1 tsp chilli powder
8 chicken thighs or 4 chicken legs
3 tbsp olive or vegetable oil
2 garlic cloves, crushed
1 large onion, chopped
1 green or red (bell) pepper, deseeded and
*   chopped*
300 ml/¹/₂ pint/1¹/₄ cups chicken stock
350 g/12 oz tomatoes, chopped
425 g/14 oz can red kidney beans, rinsed
*   and drained*
2 tbsp tomato purée (paste)
salt and pepper

1 Mix together the flour, chilli powder and seasoning in a shallow dish. Rinse the chicken, but do not dry. Dip the chicken into the seasoned flour, turning to coat it on all sides.

2 Heat the oil in a large, deep frying pan (skillet) or saucepan and add the chicken. Cook over a high heat for 3–4 minutes, turning the pieces to brown them all over. Lift the chicken out of the pan with a perforated spoon and drain on paper towels.

3 Add the garlic, onion and (bell) pepper to the pan and cook for 2–3 minutes until softened.

4 Add the stock, tomatoes, kidney beans and tomato purée (paste), stirring well. Bring to the boil, then return the chicken to the pan. Reduce the heat and simmer, covered, for about 30 minutes, until the chicken is tender. Season to taste and serve at once.

VARIATIONS

When fresh tomatoes are expensive, use a 425 g/14 oz can of chopped tomatoes instead.

Choose a mild, medium or hot variety of chilli powder, depending on your preference.

For extra intensity of flavour, use sun-dried tomato paste instead of ordinary tomato purée (paste).

STEP 1

STEP 2

STEP 3

STEP 4

BEEF GOULASH

Slow, gentle cooking is the secret to this superb goulash – it really brings out the flavour of the ingredients.

SERVES 4

2 tbsp vegetable oil
1 large onion, chopped
1 garlic clove, crushed
750 g/ 1¹/₂ lb stewing steak, cut into chunks
2 tbsp paprika
425 g/ 14 oz can chopped tomatoes
2 tbsp tomato purée (paste)
1 large red (bell) pepper, deseeded and
chopped
175 g/ 6 oz mushrooms, sliced
600 ml/ 1 pint/ 2¹/₂ cups beef stock
1 tbsp cornflour (cornstarch)
1 tbsp water
4 tbsp crème fraîche or natural yogurt
salt and pepper
paprika for sprinkling
chopped fresh parsley to garnish
long grain rice and wild rice to serve

1 Heat the oil in a large frying pan (skillet) and cook the onion and garlic for 3–4 minutes, until softened. Add the meat and cook over a high heat for 3 minutes until browned all over.

2 Add the paprika and stir well, then add the tomatoes, tomato purée (paste), (bell) pepper and mushrooms. Cook for 2 minutes, stirring frequently.

3 Pour in the stock. Bring to the boil, then reduce the heat. Cover and simmer for 1¹/₂–2 hours until the meat is very tender.

4 Blend the cornflour (cornstarch) with the water, then add to the saucepan, stirring until thickened and smooth. Cook for 1 minute, then season to taste.

5 Put the crème fraîche or natural yogurt in a bowl and sprinkle with a little paprika. Garnish the goulash with chopped parsley and serve with rice and the crème fraîche or yogurt.

PAPRIKA

Paprika is quite a mild, sweet spice, so you can add plenty without it being overpowering.

CHAPTER TWO

Pies & Bakes

❦

The beauty of cooking on a budget is that you can benefit from the wonderful flavours of slow-cooked food. Tastes and textures mellow, often improving on recipes where food is more quickly cooked. In particular, it is a way of tenderizing cheaper cuts of meat which need gentle, moist cooking to make the most of them.

In this chapter, you'll find some cheap and cheerful ways to eat a hearty meal. Choose from Mariner's Pie (see page 26) – a tasty bake where the fish is 'stretched' by combining it with other basic ingredients. Or try Bacon, Onion and Potato Hotpot (see page 32) – a surprisingly simple, delicious layered bake topped with crispy cooked bacon.

It's always a good idea to use all the available oven space when you are baking by cooking something else at the same time. It's one way of being energy-efficient and saving on fuel costs. You could even make double quantities of the chosen recipe, freezing some for future use. It hardly takes any longer to make two meals at once – and you'll have another at the ready when you next need it.

Opposite: *The extensive wheat fields of the United States.*

STEP 1

STEP 2

STEP 3

STEP 4

BAKED STUFFED ONIONS

Spanish onions are ideal for this recipe, as they have a milder, sweeter flavour that is not too overpowering.

SERVES 4

4 large Spanish onions
2 slices streaky bacon, diced
¹/₂ red (bell) pepper, deseeded and diced
125 g/4 oz lean minced (ground) beef
1 tbsp chopped mixed fresh herbs such as
*   parsley, thyme and rosemary or*
*   1 tsp dried mixed herbs*
30 g/1 oz/¹/₂ cup fresh white breadcrumbs
300 ml/¹/₂ pint/1¹/₄ cups beef stock
salt and pepper
chopped fresh parsley to garnish
long grain rice to serve

GRAVY:
30 g/1 oz/2 tbsp butter
125 g/4 oz mushrooms, chopped finely
300 ml/¹/₂ pint/1¹/₄ cups beef stock
2 tbsp cornflour (cornstarch)
2 tbsp water

1 Put the onions in a saucepan of lightly salted water. Bring to the boil then simmer for 15 minutes until tender. Drain and cool slightly, then hollow out the centres and finely chop.

2 Heat a frying pan (skillet) and cook the bacon until the fat runs. Add the chopped onion and (bell) pepper and cook for 5–7 minutes, stirring frequently.

Add the beef and cook, stirring, for 3 minutes, until browned. Remove from the heat and stir in the herbs, breadcrumbs and seasoning.

3 Grease an ovenproof dish and stand the whole onions in it. Pack the beef mixture into the centres and pour the stock around them. Bake in a preheated oven at 180°C/350°F/Gas Mark 4 for 1–1¹/₂ hours.

4 To make the gravy, heat the butter in a small saucepan and fry the mushrooms for 3–4 minutes. Strain the liquid from the onions and add to the pan with the stock. Cook for 2–3 minutes. Mix the cornflour (cornstarch) with the water then stir into the gravy and heat, stirring, until thickened and smooth. Season. Serve the onions with the gravy and rice, garnished with parsley.

VARIATION

Red, green or yellow (bell) peppers are delicious used instead of onions, but don't pre-cook them, simply discard the cores and seeds. You will still need to used chopped onion in the filling, however.

STEP 1

STEP 2

STEP 3

STEP 4

WINTER VEGETABLE COBBLER

Seasonal fresh vegetables are casseroled with lentils then topped with a ring of fresh cheese scones (biscuits) to make this tasty cobbler.

SERVES 4

1 tbsp olive oil
1 garlic clove, crushed
8 small onions, halved
2 celery sticks, sliced
250 g/8 oz swede (rutabaga), chopped
2 carrots, sliced
1/2 small cauliflower, broken into florets
250 g/8 oz mushrooms, sliced
425 g/14 oz can chopped tomatoes
60 g/2 oz/1/4 cup red lentils
2 tbsp cornflour (cornstarch)
3–4 tbsp water
300 ml/1/2 pint/1 1/4 cups vegetable stock
2 tsp Tabasco sauce
2 tsp chopped fresh oregano or parsley
oregano sprigs to garnish

COBBLER TOPPING:
250 g/8 oz/2 cups self-raising flour
60 g/2 oz/1/4 cup butter
125 g/4 oz/1 cup grated mature (sharp)
   Cheddar cheese
2 tsp chopped fresh oregano or parsley
1 egg, beaten
150 ml/1/4 pint/2/3 cup skimmed milk
salt

1 Heat the oil in a large saucepan and fry the garlic and onions for 5 minutes. Add the celery, swede (rutabaga), carrots and cauliflower and fry for 2–3 minutes.

2 Remove from the heat and add the mushrooms, tomatoes and lentils. Mix the cornflour (cornstarch) with the water and add to the pan with the vegetable stock, Tabasco sauce and oregano or parsley. Bring to the boil, stirring, until thickened. Transfer to an ovenproof dish, cover and bake in a preheated oven at 180°C/350°F/Gas Mark 4 for 20 minutes.

3 To make the topping, sift the flour and salt into a bowl. Rub in the butter, then stir in most of the cheese and the chopped herbs. Beat together the egg and milk and add enough to the dry ingredients to make a soft dough. Knead lightly, roll out to 1 cm/1/2 inch thick and cut into 5 cm/2 inch rounds.

4 Remove the casserole from the oven and increase the temperature to 200°C/400°F/Gas Mark 6. Arrange the rounds around the edge of the dish, brush with the remaining egg and milk and sprinkle with the reserved cheese. Cook for a further 10–12 minutes until the topping is risen and golden. Garnish and serve at once.

STEP 2

STEP 3

STEP 4

STEP 5

MARINER'S PIE

*Make this cheap and cheerful fish pie with coley or any other
inexpensive white fish.*

SERVES 4

*750 g/1¹/₂ lb potatoes
2 large leeks, sliced
300 ml/¹/₂ pint/1¹/₄ cups + 2 tbsp milk
1 tbsp chopped fresh parsley
60 g/2 oz/¹/₄ cup butter
60 g/2 oz/¹/₂ cup plain (all-purpose) flour
750 g/1¹/₂ lb skinned and boned coley, cut
    into chunks
1 egg
salt and pepper
chopped fresh parsley to garnish
green beans and tomatoes to serve*

1 Boil the potatoes in lightly salted
water for about 15 minutes until
tender. Meanwhile, cook the leeks in
lightly salted boiling water for about 8
minutes.

2 Drain the potatoes and leeks,
reserving the cooking liquid. Mash
the potatoes with 2 tbsp of the milk and
half the butter. Make the remaining milk
up to 600 ml/1 pint/2¹/₂ cups with the
cooking liquid from the potatoes and
leeks. Add the parsley to the milk
mixture.

3 Melt the remaining butter in a
saucepan. Add the flour and cook

gently, stirring, for 1 minute. Gradually
stir in the milk and parsley mixture.
Heat, stirring constantly, until thickened
and smooth. Season to taste.

4 Grease a large, shallow ovenproof
dish. Put the fish in the dish and
arrange the cooked leeks on top. Pour
over the parsley sauce.

5 Pipe or spoon the potatoes on top.
Bake in a preheated oven at
190°C/375°F/Gas Mark 5 for 25–30
minutes until golden. Garnish with
parsley and serve with beans and
tomatoes.

VARIATIONS

For a treat, add a few cooked, peeled
prawns (shrimp) to the fish pie.
   Top the pie with sliced potato if you
prefer – cook the potatoes until just
tender, then arrange on top of the pie,
brushing with a little beaten egg and milk.

MINCED (GROUND) LAMB & POTATO MOUSSAKA

Minced (ground) lamb makes a very tasty and authentic moussaka. For a change, use minced (ground) beef.

STEP 1

SERVES 4

1 large aubergine (eggplant), sliced
1 tbsp olive or vegetable oil
1 onion, chopped finely
1 garlic clove, crushed
350 g/12 oz minced (ground) lamb
250 g/8 oz mushrooms, sliced
425 g/14 oz can chopped tomatoes with
  herbs
150 ml/¼ pint/⅔ cup lamb or vegetable
  stock
2 tbsp cornflour (cornstarch)
2 tbsp water
500 g/1 lb potatoes, par-boiled for 10
  minutes and sliced
2 eggs
125 g/4 oz/½ cup low-fat soft cheese
150 ml/¼ pint/⅔ cup natural yogurt
60 g/2 oz/½ cup grated mature (sharp)
  Cheddar cheese
salt and pepper
flat-leaf parsley to garnish
green salad to serve

1 Lay the aubergine (eggplant) slices on a clean surface and sprinkle liberally with salt, to extract the bitter juices. Leave for 10 minutes then turn the slices over and repeat. Put in a colander, rinse and drain well.

2 Meanwhile, heat the oil in a saucepan and fry the onion and garlic for 3–4 minutes. Add the lamb and mushrooms and cook for 5 minutes, until browned. Stir in the tomatoes and stock, bring to the boil and simmer for 10 minutes. Mix the cornflour (cornstarch) with the water and stir into the pan. Cook, stirring, until thickened.

3 Spoon half the mixture into an ovenproof dish. Cover with the aubergine (eggplant) slices, then the remaining lamb mixture. Arrange the sliced potatoes on top.

4 Beat together the eggs, soft cheese, yogurt and seasoning. Pour over the potatoes to cover them completely. Sprinkle with the grated cheese.

5 Bake in a preheated oven at 190°C/375°F/Gas Mark 5 for 45 minutes until the topping is set and golden brown. Garnish with flat-leaf parsley and serve with a green salad.

STEP 2

STEP 3

STEP 4

SAVOURY BATTER PUDDINGS WITH THYME & ONION SAUCE

A variation on toad in the hole, these little puddings are filled with minced (ground) pork meatballs and served with a tasty thyme and onion sauce.

STEP 2

STEP 3

STEP 4

STEP 5

SERVES 4

2 tbsp vegetable oil
175 g/6 oz/1¹/₂ cups plain (all-purpose)
    flour
2 small eggs
450 ml/³/₄ pint/scant 2 cups milk
salt and pepper
fresh thyme sprigs to garnish
leeks and carrots to serve

FILLING:
175 g/6 oz lean minced (ground) pork
1 very small onion, chopped finely
1 small carrot, grated finely
1 tbsp chopped fresh thyme or parsley
30 g/1 oz/¹/₂ cup fresh wholemeal (whole
    wheat) breadcrumbs

SAUCE:
1 tbsp vegetable oil
1 small onion, chopped finely
125 g/4 oz button mushrooms, sliced
300 ml/¹/₂ pint/1¹/₄ cups chicken or
    vegetable stock
1 tbsp chopped fresh thyme or parsley
2 tbsp cornflour (cornstarch)
2 tbsp water

1 Spoon 2 teaspoons of the oil into each of 4 individual shallow ovenproof dishes.

2 Whisk together the flour, salt, eggs and milk to make a smooth batter. Allow to stand while making the pork filling.

3 To make the filling, mix together the pork, onion, carrot, thyme or parsley, breadcrumbs and seasoning. Form the mixture into 12 small balls and place 3 in each dish. Bake in a preheated oven at 200°C/400°F/Gas Mark 6 for 10 minutes.

4 Remove the dishes from the oven and quickly pour an equal amount of batter into each one. Bake for a further 20–25 minutes, until risen and golden brown.

5 To make the sauce, heat the oil in a saucepan and fry the onion and mushrooms until browned. Add the stock and thyme or parsley. Bring to the boil, then reduce the heat and simmer for 5 minutes. Mix the cornflour (cornstarch) with the water, stir into the pan and heat, stirring, until the sauce boils and thickens. Garnish the popovers with thyme sprigs and serve with the sauce and vegetables.

STEP 1

STEP 2

STEP 3

STEP 5

BACON, ONION & POTATO HOTPOT

Simple, straightforward and satisfying, this homely casserole is perfect for chilly winter days.

SERVES 4

60 g/2 oz/¹/₄ cup butter or margarine
1 kg/2 lb old potatoes, sliced
500 g/1 lb onions, sliced
900 ml/1¹/₂ pints/3¹/₂ cups chicken stock
500 g/1 lb streaky bacon
salt and pepper
broccoli to serve

1 Grease a 2 litre/3½ pint/2 quart casserole with some of the butter or margarine. Layer the potatoes and onions alternately in the casserole dish, seasoning each layer. Finish with a layer of potatoes.

2 Pour the stock over the potatoes and dot the surface with the remaining butter or margarine. Cover and bake in a preheated oven at 190°C/375°F/Gas Mark 5 for 45 minutes.

3 Remove the lid from the casserole and return to the oven for a further 30 minutes until the potatoes are golden brown.

4 Meanwhile, cook the bacon under a preheated moderate grill (broiler) until cooked, but not too crisp.

5 Put the bacon on top of the potatoes and cook in the oven for a further 10 minutes. Serve at once on warmed plates, with broccoli.

ACCOMPANIMENTS

As an alternative to broccoli, hot, buttered cabbage seasoned with a pinch of nutmeg tastes just right with this tasty, economical hotpot.

Homemade chutney or relish can also be served with this dish.

CHAPTER THREE

Pasta, Rice & Grains

❧

Pasta, grains, rice and noodles are the carbohydrate foods that fill us up and provide the slow release of energy that gets us through the day. Gone are the days when people thought these starchy foods were fattening. Now people realize that carbohydrates – the fuel store in plants – can be our own fuel supply too, so foods such as pasta, potatoes, grains and rice form an important basic item for each and every one of our meals.

In themselves, these foods are quite bland, which means that they can so easily take on the flavours and characteristics of many different meals. Think of the innumerable ways in which the Italians serve pasta, for example. This chapter will show you a little of the versatility of these foods, so you can continue to experiment in your own kitchen and develop some ideas of your own.

Opposite: *A view over Florence, dominated by the magnificent dome of the cathedral.*

STEP 1

STEP 2

STEP 3

STEP 4

THAI-STYLE CHICKEN FRIED RICE

A few authentic ingredients give this spicy rice dish a typically Thai flavour.

SERVES 4

250 g/8 oz/generous 1 cup long-grain rice
4 tbsp vegetable oil
2 garlic cloves, chopped finely
6 shallots, sliced finely
1 red (bell) pepper, deseeded and diced
125 g/4 oz green beans, cut into 2.5 cm/
*   1 inch lengths*
1 tbsp Thai red curry paste
350 g/12 oz cooked chicken, chopped
½ tsp ground coriander
1 tsp finely grated ginger root
2 tbsp Thai fish sauce
finely grated rind of 1 lime
3 tbsp lime juice
1 tbsp chopped fresh coriander (cilantro)
salt and pepper

TO GARNISH:
lime wedges
fresh coriander (cilantro) sprigs

1 Cook the rice in plenty of boiling, lightly salted water for 12–15 minutes until tender. Drain, rinse in cold water and drain thoroughly.

2 Heat the oil in a large frying pan (skillet) or wok and add the garlic and shallots. Fry gently for 2–3 minutes until golden.

3 Add the (bell) pepper and green beans and stir-fry for 2 minutes. Add the Thai curry paste and stir-fry for 1 minute.

4 Add the cooked rice to the pan then add the chicken, ground coriander, ginger, fish sauce, lime rind and juice and fresh coriander (cilantro). Stir-fry over a medium-high heat for about 4–5 minutes, until the rice and chicken are thoroughly reheated. Season to taste.

5 Garnish with lime wedges and coriander (cilantro) and serve.

THAI RED CURRY PASTE

Thai red curry paste can be bought in small jars in supermarkets and delicatessens. Look for it in the Oriental foods section.

THAI FISH SAUCE

Thai fish sauce is used to season many Thai dishes. It adds a salty flavour, rather than a seafood one, so take care when adding extra salt to the dish. Use light soy sauce as an alternative.

STEP 1

STEP 2

STEP 3

STEP 4

MUSHROOM & PARMESAN RISOTTO

Make this creamy risotto with Italian arborio rice and freshly grated Parmesan cheese for the best results.

SERVES 4

2 tbsp olive or vegetable oil
250 g/8 oz/generous 1 cup arborio (risotto)
    rice
2 garlic cloves, crushed
1 onion, chopped
2 celery sticks, chopped
1 red or green (bell) pepper, deseeded and
    chopped
250 g/8 oz mushrooms, sliced
1 tbsp chopped fresh oregano or 1 tsp dried
    oregano
1 litre/1 3/4 pints/4 cups vegetable stock
60 g /2 oz sun-dried tomatoes in olive oil,
    drained and chopped (optional)
60 g/2 oz/1/2 cup finely grated Parmesan
    cheese
salt and pepper

TO GARNISH:
fresh flat-leaf parsley sprigs
fresh bay leaves

1 Heat the oil in a wok or large frying pan (skillet). Add the rice and cook, stirring, for 5 minutes.

2 Add the garlic, onion, celery and (bell) pepper and cook, stirring, for 5 minutes. Add the mushrooms and cook for a further 3–4 minutes.

3 Stir in the oregano and stock. Heat until just boiling, then reduce the heat, cover and simmer gently for about 20 minutes until the rice is tender and creamy.

4 Add the sun-dried tomatoes, if using, and season to taste. Stir in half the Parmesan cheese. Top with the remaining cheese, garnish with flat-leaf parsley and bay leaves and serve.

ARBORIO RICE

This is an Italian short-grain rice used specially for risottos – the starch it contains is essential for the creamy texture, so don't rinse it before cooking.
   Check the rice as it cooks from time to time. If it has absorbed all the liquid before it is tender, add a little extra stock or water.

OIL

Use the oil from the sun-dried tomatoes to fry the rice to give it extra flavour.

STEP 1

PASTA WITH PINE NUTS (KERNELS) & BLUE CHEESE

Simple, quick and inexpensive, this tasty pasta dish can be prepared in minutes.

SERVES 4

60 g/2 oz/1 cup pine nuts (kernels)
350 g/12 oz dried pasta shapes
2 courgettes (zucchini), sliced
125 g/4 oz broccoli, broken into florets
200 g/7 oz/1 cup full-fat soft cheese
150 ml/¼ pint/⅔ cup milk
1 tbsp chopped fresh basil
125 g/4 oz button mushrooms, sliced
90 g/3 oz Stilton or Danish blue cheese,
  crumbled
salt and pepper
sprigs of fresh basil to garnish
green salad to serve

1 Scatter the pine nuts (kernels) on to a baking sheet and grill (broil), turning occasionally, until lightly browned all over. Set aside.

2 Cook the pasta in plenty of boiling, lightly salted water for 8–10 minutes until just tender. Meanwhile, cook the courgettes (zucchini) and broccoli in a small amount of boiling, lightly salted water for about 5 minutes until just tender.

3 Put the soft cheese into a saucepan and heat gently, stirring constantly. Add the milk and stir to mix.

4 Add the basil and mushrooms and cook gently for 2–3 minutes. Stir in the blue cheese and season to taste.

5 Drain the pasta and the vegetables and mix together. Pour over the cheese and mushroom sauce and add the pine nuts (kernels). Toss gently to mix. Garnish with basil sprigs and serve on warmed plates with a green salad.

PASTA

Avoid overcooking pasta; it should retain a little 'bite' (known as 'al dente' in Italian).

LOW-FAT VERSION

Use low-fat soft cheese instead of full-fat soft cheese if you want to reduce the calories and fat of this recipe.

STEP 2

STEP 3

STEP 4

STEP 1

STEP 2

STEP 3

STEP 4

SMOKED FISH LASAGNE

*Use smoked cod or haddock in this delicious lasagne. It's a great way to
make a little go a long way.*

SERVES 4

2 tsp olive or vegetable oil
1 garlic clove, crushed
1 small onion, chopped finely
125 g/4 oz mushrooms, sliced
425 g/14 oz can chopped tomatoes
1 small courgette (zucchini), sliced
150 ml/^{1}/$_4$ pint/^{2}/$_3$ cup vegetable stock or
    water
30 g/1 oz/2 tbsp butter or margarine
300 ml/^{1}/$_2$ pint/1^1/$_4$ cups skimmed milk
30 g/1 oz/^{1}/$_4$ cup plain (all-purpose) flour
125 g/4 oz/1 cup grated mature (sharp)
    Cheddar cheese
1 tbsp chopped fresh parsley
125 g/4 oz (6 sheets) pre-cooked lasagne
350 g/12 oz skinned and boned smoked cod
    or haddock, cut into chunks
salt and pepper
fresh parsley sprigs to garnish

1 Heat the oil in a saucepan and fry
the garlic and onion for about 5
minutes. Add the mushrooms and cook
for 3 minutes.

2 Add the tomatoes, courgette
(zucchini) and stock or water and
simmer, uncovered, for 15–20 minutes
until the vegetables are soft. Season.

3 Put the butter or margarine, milk
and flour into a small saucepan and
heat, whisking constantly, until the
sauce boils and thickens. Remove from
the heat and add half the cheese and all
the parsley. Stir gently to melt the cheese
and season to taste.

4 Spoon the tomato sauce mixture
into a large, shallow ovenproof dish
and top with half the lasagne sheets.
Scatter the chunks of fish evenly over the
top, then pour over half the cheese sauce.
Top with the remaining lasagne sheets
and spread the rest of the cheese sauce on
top. Sprinkle with the remaining cheese.

5 Bake in a preheated oven at
190°C/375°F/Gas Mark 5 for 40
minutes, until the top is golden brown
and bubbling. Garnish with parsley
sprigs and serve.

BUYING FISH

Look out for bargains at your fishmongers,
and substitute whatever fish is cheapest.
Firm white fish is particularly suitable for
this recipe.

STEP 1

STEP 2

STEP 3

STEP 4

QUICK CHINESE CHICKEN
WITH NOODLES

*Chicken and fresh vegetables are flavoured with ginger and Chinese
five-spice powder in this speedy stir-fry.*

SERVES 4

175 g/6 oz Chinese thread egg noodles
2 tbsp sesame or vegetable oil
30 g/1 oz/¹/₄ cup peanuts
1 bunch of spring onions (scallions), sliced
*1 green (bell) pepper, deseeded and cut into
    thin strips*
1 large carrot, cut into matchsticks
*125 g/4 oz cauliflower, broken into small
    florets*
*350 g/12 oz skinless, boneless chicken, cut
    into strips*
250 g/8 oz mushrooms, sliced
1 tsp finely grated ginger root
1 tsp Chinese five-spice powder
1 tbsp chopped fresh coriander (cilantro)
1 tbsp light soy sauce
salt and pepper
fresh chives to garnish

1 Put the noodles into a large bowl
and cover with boiling water.
Leave to soak for 6 minutes, or according
to packet instructions.

2 Meanwhile, heat the oil in a wok or
large frying pan (skillet). Add the
peanuts and stir-fry for about 1 minute
until browned. Lift them out with a
perforated spoon and drain on paper
towels.

3 Add the spring onions (scallions),
(bell) pepper, carrot, cauliflower
and chicken to the pan. Stir-fry over a
high heat for 4–5 minutes, until the
chicken is cooked. The vegetables should
remain crisp and colourful.

4 Drain the noodles thoroughly and
add them to the wok. Add the
mushrooms and stir-fry for 2 minutes.
Add the ginger, five-spice powder and
coriander (cilantro) and stir-fry for 1
more minute.

5 Season with soy sauce and salt and
pepper. Sprinkle with the peanuts,
garnish with chives and serve on
warmed plates.

VARIATIONS

Instead of ginger root, ¹/₂ teaspoon
ground ginger can be used.
  Vary the vegetables according to what
is in season. Make the most of bargains
bought from your greengrocer or market.

STEP 1

STEP 2

STEP 3

STEP 4

MOROCCAN VEGETABLE COUSCOUS

Couscous is a semolina grain which is very quick to cook, and it makes a pleasant change from rice or pasta.

SERVES 4

2 tbsp vegetable oil
1 large onion, chopped coarsely
1 carrot, chopped
1 turnip, chopped
600 ml/ 1 pint/ 2½ cups vegetable stock
175 g/6 oz/ 1 cup couscous
2 tomatoes, skinned and quartered
2 courgettes (zucchini), chopped
1 red (bell) pepper, deseeded and chopped
125 g/4 oz green beans, chopped
grated rind of 1 lemon
pinch of ground turmeric (optional)
1 tbsp finely chopped fresh coriander
   (cilantro) or parsley
salt and pepper
fresh flat-leaf parsley sprigs to garnish

1 Heat the oil in a large saucepan and fry the onion, carrot and turnip for 3–4 minutes. Add the vegetable stock and bring to the boil. Cover and simmer gently for about 20 minutes.

2 Meanwhile, put the couscous in a bowl and moisten with a little boiling water, stirring, until the grains have swollen and separated.

3 Add the tomatoes, courgettes (zucchini), (bell) pepper and green beans to the saucepan.

4 Stir the lemon rind and turmeric, if using, into the couscous and mix well. Put the couscous in a steamer and position over the vegetables. Simmer the vegetables so that the couscous steams for 8–10 minutes.

5 Pile the couscous onto warmed serving plates. Ladle the vegetables and some of the liquid on top. Scatter with the coriander (cilantro) or parsley and serve at once, garnished with parsley sprigs.

VARIATION

For a tasty chicken couscous, cook 4 chicken joints with the vegetables in step 1, adding extra stock to cover.

TIP

Add extra stock to the vegetables if the saucepan begins to boil dry.

CHAPTER FOUR

Eggs & Cheese

❧

Eggs and cheese are the two great staple foods of low-cost cookery. High in protein yet relatively inexpensive, they can form the foundation of many tasty budget meals.

Eggs are so versatile. From simple boiled, poached, scrambled and fried eggs you can progress to quick and tasty omelettes through to light and impressive soufflés. Eggs form one of the vital ingredients in many basic recipes – batter, choux pastry and custards to name but a few.

With the recipes in this chapter, for example, you can rustle up Savoury Bread and Butter Pudding (see page 52) in a matter of moments for a speedy mid-week meal – the hot melting cheese makes your mouth water as the pudding emerges from the oven, all puffed-up and golden brown. Or try Egg and Chick-Pea (Garbanzo Bean) Curry (see page 50) – the subtle spices will soon perk up your appetite!

Opposite: *A cheese market in Holland. The whole cheeses are still transported in the traditional way.*

STEP 1

STEP 2

STEP 3

STEP 4

EGG & CHICK-PEA (GARBANZO BEAN) CURRY

This easy vegetarian curry is always enjoyed. Double the quantities and it's a great dish if you're cooking for a crowd.

SERVES 4

2 tbsp vegetable oil
2 garlic cloves, crushed
1 large onion, chopped
1 large carrot, sliced
1 apple, cored and chopped
2 tbsp medium-hot curry powder
1 tsp finely grated fresh ginger root
2 tsp paprika
900 ml/ 1 ^{1}/$_2$ pints/ 3 ^{1}/$_2$ cups vegetable stock
2 tbsp tomato purée (paste)
^{1}/$_2$ small cauliflower, broken into florets
475 g/ 15 oz can chick-peas (garbanzo
    beans), rinsed and drained
30 g/ 1 oz/ 2 tbsp sultanas (golden raisins)
    or raisins
2 tbsp cornflour (cornstarch)
2 tbsp water
4 hard-boiled (hard-cooked) eggs, quartered
salt and pepper
paprika to garnish

CUCUMBER DIP:
7.5 cm/ 3 inch piece of cucumber, chopped
    finely
1 tbsp chopped fresh mint
150 ml/ ^{1}/$_4$ pint/ ^{2}/$_3$ cup natural yogurt
sprigs of fresh mint to garnish

1 Heat the oil in a large saucepan
and fry the garlic, onion, carrot
and apple for 4–5 minutes, until
softened.

2 Add the curry powder, ginger and
paprika and fry for 1 minute more.

3 Stir in the vegetable stock and
tomato purée (paste).

4 Add the cauliflower, chick-peas
(garbanzo beans) and sultanas
(golden raisins) or raisins. Bring to the
boil, then reduce the heat and simmer,
covered, for 25–30 minutes until the
vegetables are tender.

5 Blend the cornflour (cornstarch)
with the water and add to the
curry, stirring until thickened. Cook
gently for 2 minutes. Season to taste.

6 To make the dip, in a small serving
bowl, mix together the cucumber,
mint and yogurt.

7 Ladle the curry onto 4 warmed
serving plates and arrange the eggs
on top. Sprinkle with a little paprika.
Garnish the cucumber and mint dip with
mint and serve with the curry.

STEP 1

STEP 2

STEP 3

STEP 4

SAVOURY BREAD & BUTTER PUDDING

Quick, simple and nutritious – what more could you ask for an inexpensive mid-week meal?

SERVES 4

60 g/2 oz/¼ cup butter or margarine
1 bunch spring onions (scallions), sliced
6 slices of white or brown bread, crusts removed
175g/6 oz/1½ cups grated mature (sharp) Cheddar cheese
2 eggs
450 ml/¾ pint/scant 2 cups milk
salt and pepper
fresh flat-leaf parsley sprigs to garnish

1 Grease a 1.5 litre/2½ pint/1½ quart baking dish with a little of the butter or margarine. Melt the remaining butter or margarine in a small saucepan and fry the spring onions (scallions) until softened and golden.

2 Meanwhile, cut the bread into triangles and layer half of them in the baking dish. Top with the spring onions (scallions) and half the cheese.

3 Beat together the eggs and milk and season with salt and pepper. Layer the remaining triangles of bread in the dish and carefully pour over the milk mixture. Leave to soak for 15–20 minutes.

4 Sprinkle the remaining cheese over the soaked bread pudding. Bake in a preheated oven at 190°C/375°F/Gas Mark 5 for 35–40 minutes until puffed up and golden brown. Garnish with flat-leaf parsley and serve at once.

BREAD

This is an excellent recipe for using up bread that is slightly stale.

VARIATIONS

For a change, add 60 g/2 oz/⅓ cup chopped cooked ham to the spring onions (scallions), when layering them in the baking dish.

Use 1 large onion instead of the spring onions (scallions), if preferred.

SPINACH & CHEESE PANCAKE STACK

Make a pile of pancakes, then bake them with a wonderful filling for a satisfying and nutritious meal.

STEP 1

SERVES 4

125 g/4 oz/1 cup plain (all-purpose) flour
1 egg
300 ml/½ pint/1¼ cups milk
2 tbsp vegetable oil
salt and pepper
fresh flat-leaf parsley sprigs to garnish
mixed salad to serve

FILLING:
500 g/1 lb fresh spinach, washed
   thoroughly
1 onion, chopped
2 garlic cloves, crushed
425 g/14 oz can chopped tomatoes
1 tsp mixed dried Italian herbs
125 g/4 oz/1 cup grated mature (sharp)
   Cheddar cheese

1 Sift the flour and a pinch of salt into a large bowl. Add the egg and milk and whisk together to make a smooth batter.

2 Reserve 1 tablespoon of the oil. Heat a large heavy-based frying pan (skillet) and make 4 pancakes with the batter, using a few drops of oil to make each one. Stack the pancakes on a plate once they are cooked.

3 To make the filling, pack the spinach into a large saucepan and add a little salted water. Cover and cook for 4–5 minutes, then drain well and squeeze out the excess liquid.

4 Heat the reserved oil in a frying pan (skillet) and fry the onion and garlic for 5 minutes. Add the tomatoes and cook for about 10 minutes until pulpy. Add the mixed herbs and season to taste.

5 Brush a 23 cm/9 inch deep cake tin (pan) with the remaining oil.

6 Layer the pancakes, spinach and tomato mixture in the tin (pan), finishing with a pancake. Scatter the cheese evenly over the surface and bake in a preheated oven at 190°C/375°F/Gas Mark 5 for 30 minutes until golden brown. Slice into wedges, garnish and serve hot with a mixed salad.

STEP 2

STEP 3

VARIATIONS

Use wholemeal (whole wheat) flour instead of white flour for the pancakes.
  Add some sliced mushrooms to the tomato mixture if you wish.

STEP 4

55

STEP 1

STEP 2

STEP 4

STEP 5

CHICKEN & SWEETCORN PUFF

*This delicious choux puff is an impressive dish yet it's simple to make.
You can use the choux pastry as a topping for all kinds of filling.*

SERVES 4

CHOUX PASTRY:
75 g/2½ oz/generous ½ cup plain (all-
purpose) flour
60 g /2 oz/¼ cup butter or block margarine
150 ml/¼ pint/⅔ cup water
2 eggs, beaten
salt

FILLING:
30 g/1 oz/2 tbsp butter or block margarine
30 g/1 oz/¼ cup plain (all-purpose) flour
300 ml/½ pint/1¼ cups skimmed milk
250 g/8 oz/1 cup cooked chicken, shredded
125 g/4 oz/¾ cup canned sweetcorn,
drained
1 tbsp chopped fresh parsley
salt and pepper

1 To make the choux pastry, sift the
flour and salt into a bowl. Put the
butter or margarine and water into a
saucepan, then heat gently to melt. Bring
to the boil. Remove from the heat and
quickly add the flour all at once. Beat
with a wooden spoon until the mixture
leaves the sides of the saucepan clean.
Leave to cool slightly.

2 Gradually beat in the eggs, using
an electric whisk if wished, until

the mixture is thick and very glossy. Chill
while making the filling.

3 To make the filling, put the butter
or margarine, flour and milk into a
saucepan. Heat, whisking constantly,
until smooth and thickened.

4 Add the chicken, sweetcorn and
parsley to the sauce. Season to
taste. Pour into a 1 litre/1¾ pint/4 cup
shallow baking dish.

5 Spoon the choux pastry around the
edge of the dish. Bake in a
preheated oven at 220°C/425°F/Gas
Mark 7 for 35–40 minutes until puffed
up and golden brown. Serve at once.

CHOUX PASTRY

For successful choux pastry, it is
important to measure the ingredients
accurately. Make sure the mixture has
cooled before beating in the eggs, or they
could curdle.

STEP 1

STEP 3

STEP 4

STEP 5

GOLDEN CHEESE & LEEK POTATO CAKES

Make these tasty potato cakes for a quick and simple supper dish. Serve them with scrambled eggs if you're very hungry.

SERVES 4

1 kg/ 2 lb potatoes
4 tbsp milk
60 g/ 2 oz/ 1/4 cup butter or margarine
2 leeks, chopped finely
1 onion, chopped finely
175 g/ 6 oz/ 1 1/2 cups grated Caerphilly or
    Cheddar cheese
1 tbsp chopped fresh parsley or chives
1 egg, beaten
2 tbsp water
90 g/ 3 oz/ 1 1/2 cups fresh white or brown
    breadcrumbs
vegetable oil for shallow frying
salt and pepper
fresh flat-leaf parsley sprigs to garnish
mixed salad to serve

1 Cook the potatoes in lightly salted boiling water until tender. Drain and mash them with the milk and the butter or margarine.

2 Cook the leeks and onion in a small amount of salted boiling water for about 10 minutes until tender. Drain.

3 In a large mixing bowl, combine the leeks and onion with the mashed potato, cheese and parsley or chives. Season to taste.

4 Beat together the egg and water in a shallow bowl. Sprinkle the breadcrumbs into a separate shallow bowl. Shape the potato mixture into 12 even-sized cakes, brushing each with the egg mixture, then coating with the breadcrumbs.

5 Heat the oil in a large frying pan (skillet) and fry the potato cakes gently for about 2–3 minutes on each side until light golden brown. Garnish with flat-leaf parsley and serve with a mixed salad.

FISH CAKES

Transform these potato cakes into tasty fish cakes by mixing in a 200 g/7 oz can of tuna, drained and flaked.

POTATOES

This is an excellent recipe for using up leftover mashed potatoes.

STEP 1

STEP 2

STEP 3

STEP 4

FLAMENCO EGGS

This Spanish-style egg recipe is full of lively colours and flavours.
Eating on a budget need never be dull.

SERVES 4

6 tbsp olive oil
2 thick slices white bread, cut into cubes
500 g/1 lb potatoes, cut into small cubes
1 onion, chopped
60 g/2 oz green beans, cut into ¹/₂ cm/1 inch
    lengths
2 small courgettes (zucchini), halved and
    sliced
1 red (bell) pepper, deseeded and chopped
4 tomatoes, deseeded and sliced
2 chorizo sausages, sliced
chilli powder, to taste
4 eggs
salt
chopped fresh parsley to garnish

1 Heat the oil in a large frying pan
(skillet) and add the cubes of bread.
Fry until golden brown, then remove
with a perforated spoon and drain on
paper towels. Set aside.

2 Add the potatoes to the frying pan
(skillet) and cook over a low heat,
turning often, for about 15 minutes until
just tender.

3 Add the onion to the frying pan
(skillet) and cook for 3 minutes,
then add the green beans, courgettes

(zucchini), (bell) pepper and tomatoes.
Cook gently for 3–4 minutes, stirring
often. Stir in the chorizo sausage. Season
with salt and a little chilli powder.

4 Grease 4 individual ovenproof
dishes or 1 large ovenproof dish
with olive oil. Transfer the vegetable
mixture to the dishes and make a hollow
in the mixture. Carefully crack 1 egg into
each hollow. Bake in a preheated oven at
190°C/375°F/Gas Mark 5 for 10
minutes.

5 Sprinkle the cubes of fried bread
over the surface and bake for a
further 2 minutes. Serve immediately,
garnished with chopped fresh parsley.

CHILLI POWDER

If you don't like the heat of chilli powder,
use freshly ground black pepper instead.

TIP

Slightly stale bread is best for making the
fried bread cubes, as it absorbs less oil.

CHAPTER FIVE

Desserts

❧

This chapter is for everyone who feels that they haven't finished a meal properly until they have eaten dessert. And why not? Puddings are such a delight and great for filling any gaps. Lots of people prefer not to eat puddings, believing them to be stodgy and unhealthy, but this need not be the case. The key to a healthy, balanced diet is moderation, which doesn't mean banning foods that you love to eat. Every now and again a delicious dessert can be just what you need to feel comforted and cosy.

As with all the ideas in this book, the recipes have been developed with cost-cutting in mind. The recipes use basic, store-cupboard foods or ingredients that can easily be bought locally – nothing exotic or expensive. And there is nothing complicated in the preparation either – the puddings are quick and simple to prepare, which means that they are just right for any occasion. So whether it's for a family lunch or a special party, you can be sure that these desserts will go down a treat.

Opposite: *Fresh fruits are so packed with flavour you don't need to add lots of other ingredients to make mouthwatering desserts.*

STEP 1

STEP 2

STEP 3

STEP 4

CHOCOLATE BREAD PUDDING

This chocolate pudding is served with hot fudge sauce, making it the most delicious way to use up bread that is slightly stale.

SERVES 4

6 thick slices white bread, crusts removed
450 ml/³/₄ pint/2 cups milk
175 g/6 oz can evaporated milk
2 tbsp unsweetened cocoa powder
2 eggs
30 g/1 oz/2 tbsp dark muscovado sugar
1 tsp vanilla flavouring (extract)
icing (confectioners') sugar for dusting

HOT FUDGE SAUCE:
60 g/2 oz/2 squares dark chocolate, broken
  into pieces
1 tbsp unsweetened cocoa powder
2 tbsp golden (light corn) syrup
60 g/2 oz/¹/₄ cup butter or margarine
30 g/1 oz/2 tbsp dark muscovado sugar
150 ml/¹/₄ pint/²/₃ cup milk
1 tbsp cornflour (cornstarch)

1 Grease a shallow ovenproof dish. Cut the bread into squares and layer them in the dish.

2 Heat the milk, evaporated milk and cocoa powder until lukewarm, stirring occasionally.

3 Whisk together the eggs, sugar and vanilla flavouring (extract). Add the warm milk mixture and beat well.

4 Pour into the baking dish, making sure that all the bread is covered. Cover the dish with clingfilm (plastic wrap) and chill for 1–2 hours.

5 Bake the pudding in a preheated oven at 180°C/350°F/Gas Mark 4 for about 35–40 minutes until set. Allow to stand for 5 minutes.

6 To make the sauce, put the chocolate, cocoa powder, syrup, butter or margarine, sugar, milk and cornflour (cornstarch) into a saucepan. Heat gently, stirring until smooth.

7 Dust the pudding with icing (confectioners') sugar and serve with the hot fudge sauce.

TIPS

The bread can be left to soak in the chocolate mixture for several hours, or overnight, if preferred.

STEP 1

STEP 2

STEP 3

STEP 4

QUICK SYRUP SPONGE

You won't believe your eyes when you see how quickly this sponge pudding cooks!

SERVES 4

125 g/4 oz/¹⁄₂ cup butter or margarine
4 tbsp golden (light corn) syrup
90 g/3 oz/¹⁄₃ cup caster (superfine) sugar
2 eggs
125 g/4 oz/1 cup self-raising flour
1 tsp baking powder
about 2 tbsp warm water
custard to serve

1 Grease a 1.5 litre/2½ pint/ 1½ quart pudding basin (mold) with a small amount of the butter or margarine. Spoon the syrup into the basin (mold).

2 Cream the remaining butter or margarine with the sugar until light and fluffy. Gradually add the eggs, beating well between each addition.

3 Sift the flour and baking powder together, then fold into the creamed mixture using a large metal spoon. Add enough water to give a soft, dropping consistency. Spoon into the pudding basin (mold) and level the surface.

4 Cover with microwave-safe film, leaving a small space to allow air to

escape. Microwave on Full Power for 4 minutes, then remove from the microwave and allow the pudding to stand for 5 minutes, while it continues to cook.

5 Turn the pudding out onto a serving plate. Serve with custard.

STEAMING

If you don't have a microwave, this pudding can be steamed. Cover the pudding with a piece of pleated baking parchment then a piece of pleated foil, secure with string and place in a large saucepan. Add enough boiling water to come halfway up the sides of the basin (mold), cover and steam for 1¹⁄₂ hours, topping up with more boiling water as necessary.

GOLDEN (LIGHT CORN) SYRUP

Warm the spoon that you use to measure out the syrup and the syrup will slip off the spoon quite easily.
 Use your favourite jam in place of golden (light corn) syrup for a change.

STEP 1

STEP 2

STEP 3

STEP 4

PANCAKES WITH APPLES & BUTTERSCOTCH SAUCE

The sharpness of the apples contrasts with the sweetness of the sauce in this mouthwatering pancake recipe.

SERVES 4

125 g/4 oz/1 cup plain (all-purpose) flour
1 tsp finely grated lemon rind
1 egg
300 ml/¹/₂ pint/1¹/₄ cups milk
1–2 tbsp vegetable oil
salt
pared lemon rind to garnish

FILLING:
250 g/8 oz cooking apples, peeled, cored and sliced
30 g/1 oz/2 tbsp sultanas (golden raisins)

SAUCE:
90 g/3 oz/¹/₃ cup butter
3 tbsp golden (light corn) syrup
90 g/3 oz/¹/₂ cup light muscovado sugar
1 tbsp rum or brandy (optional)
1 tbsp lemon juice

1 Sift the flour and salt into a large mixing bowl. Add the lemon rind, egg and milk and whisk together to make a smooth batter.

2 Heat a few drops of oil in a heavy-based frying pan (skillet). Make 8 thin pancakes, using a few drops of oil for each one. Stack the cooked pancakes, layering them with paper towels.

3 To make the filling, cook the apples with the sultanas (golden raisins) in a little water until soft. Divide the mixture between the pancakes and roll up or fold into triangles. Place them in a buttered ovenproof dish and bake in a preheated oven at 160°C/325°F/Gas Mark 3 for 15 minutes to warm through.

4 To make the sauce, melt the butter, syrup and sugar together in a saucepan, stirring well. Add the rum or brandy, if using, and the lemon juice. Do not allow the mixture to boil.

5 Serve the pancakes on warm plates, with a little sauce poured over and garnished with lemon rind.

TIPS

If the apples are quite tart, sweeten them with a little sugar.
To make thin pancakes, tilt the pan as the batter is added, so that it flows quickly over the base.

STEP 1

STEP 4

STEP 5

STEP 6

APRICOT & BANANA QUEEN OF PUDDINGS

A scrumptious version of a classic British pudding.

SERVES 4

125 g/4 oz/2 cups fresh white breadcrumbs
600 ml/1 pint/2¹/₂ cups milk
3 eggs
¹/₂ tsp vanilla flavouring (extract)
60 g/2 oz/¹/₄ cup caster (superfine) sugar
2 bananas
1 tbsp lemon juice
3 tbsp apricot jam

1 Sprinkle the breadcrumbs into a 1 litre/1¾ pint/4 cup ovenproof dish. Heat the milk until lukewarm, then pour it over the breadcrumbs.

2 Separate 2 of the eggs and beat the yolks with the remaining whole egg. Add to the baking dish with the vanilla flavouring (extract) and half the sugar, stirring well to mix. Allow to stand for 10 minutes.

3 Bake in a preheated oven at 180°C/350°F/Gas Mark 4 for 40 minutes until set. Remove from the oven.

4 Slice the bananas and sprinkle with the lemon juice. Spoon the apricot jam on to the pudding and spread out to cover the surface. Arrange the bananas on top of the apricot jam.

5 Whisk the egg whites until stiff, then add the remaining sugar. Whisk until very stiff and glossy.

6 Pile on top of the pudding, return to the oven and cook for a further 10–15 minutes until set and golden brown. Serve immediately.

MERINGUE

The meringue will have a soft, marshmallow-like texture, unlike a hard meringue which is cooked slowly for 2–3 hours until dry.

Always use a grease-free bowl and whisk for beating egg-whites, otherwise they will not whip properly.

BAKED SEMOLINA PUDDING WITH SPICED PLUMS

Plums simmered in orange juice and mixed spice complement this semolina pudding perfectly.

STEP 1

SERVES 4

30 g/1 oz/2 tbsp butter or margarine
600 ml/1 pint/2½ cups milk
finely pared rind and juice of 1 orange
60 g/2 oz/⅓ cup semolina
pinch of grated nutmeg
30 g/1 oz/2 tbsp caster (superfine) sugar
1 egg, beaten

TO SERVE:
knob of butter
grated nutmeg

SPICED PLUMS:
250 g/8 oz plums, halved and stoned
150 ml/¼ pint/⅔ cup orange juice
30 g/1 oz/2 tbsp caster (superfine) sugar
½ tsp ground mixed spice

1 Grease a 1 litre/1¾ pint/4 cup ovenproof dish with a little of the butter or margarine. Put the milk, the remaining butter or margarine and the orange rind in a saucepan. Sprinkle in the semolina and heat until boiling, stirring constantly. Simmer gently for 2–3 minutes. Remove from the heat.

2 Add the nutmeg, orange juice and sugar to the semolina mixture, stirring well. Add the egg and stir to mix.

3 Transfer the mixture to the prepared dish and bake in a preheated oven at 190°C/375°F/Gas Mark 5 for about 30 minutes until lightly browned.

4 To make the spiced plums, put the plums, orange juice, sugar and spice into a saucepan and simmer gently for about 10 minutes until just tender. Leave to cool slightly.

5 Top the semolina pudding with a knob of butter and grated nutmeg and serve with the spiced plums.

VARIATION

Stewed apples make a delicious alternative to plums.

TIP

If you are short of time, there is no need to bake the pudding. Just reheat it gently, stirring constantly, after adding the egg.

STEP 2

STEP 3

STEP 4

STEP 1

STEP 2

STEP 3

STEP 4

COFFEE CREAM TRIFLE

Make the most of leftover ginger cake with this wonderful trifle that's perfect for a special occasion.

SERVES 6

175 g/6 oz ginger cake, sliced
3 tbsp coffee essence
5 tbsp hot water
4 tbsp dark rum
60 g/2 oz/¹/₃ cup cornflour (cornstarch)
60 g/2 oz/3 tbsp light muscovado sugar
15 g/¹/₂ oz/1 tbsp butter or margarine
600 ml/1 pint/2¹/₂ cups milk
150 ml/¹/₄ pint/²/₃ cup whipping (heavy) cream

TO DECORATE:
1 tbsp demerara (brown crystal) sugar
grated chocolate
flaked almonds

1 Arrange the slices of ginger cake in the base of a glass serving dish. Mix together the coffee essence, water and rum. Pour half over the ginger cake.

2 Put the cornflour (cornstarch), sugar, butter or margarine and milk in a saucepan. Heat gently, whisking constantly until thickened and smooth. Cook gently for 2 minutes. Remove from the heat.

3 Add the remaining coffee mixture, stirring well to blend. Pour over the ginger cake. Allow to cool completely.

4 In a large chilled bowl, whip the cream until it holds its shape. Spoon into a large piping bag fitted with a star nozzle (tip).

5 Pipe swirls of cream around the edge of the trifle. Sprinkle with demerara (brown crystal) sugar and decorate with grated chocolate and flaked almonds.

VARIATIONS

Use plain sponge cake instead of ginger cake, if preferred.

To make this trifle more economical, use 2 teaspoons rum essence in place of the rum.

KEEPING TO A BUDGET

BAKING CAKES

Some of the costliest items to buy are the snacks, biscuits (cookies), cakes, bakes and puddings that are so tempting, and that make great fillers when you're feeling hungry. So if you enjoy eating them, you're sure to enjoy making them too. Set aside an afternoon when you can batch-bake some cakes to eat over a few weeks, and keep them well-wrapped in an airtight container or freeze them until you need them.

If you are batch-baking, it is best to choose cakes that need the same oven temperature, so that you are making the most economical use of both your time and the oven heat.

Make lots of snack foods for the children; perfect for picnics and packed lunches. They will love homemade flapjacks and cookies, and they will be far cheaper than bought varieties or snack bars and chocolate.

Homemade pastry (pie dough) is much cheaper than the bought variety, but it can get tedious if you have to make it from scratch each time. Why not do the rubbing in for several batches of shortcrust pastry (basic pie dough) at once, then bag them in portions. You can keep them in the refrigerator for 3–4 weeks, or freeze them for 3 months.

Cooking on a budget can be quite a challenge – it's not an easy task making the money stretch when everything is so expensive. Yet there are many ways to cut down on your expenditure, once you've got into the swing of watching the purse strings!

The most important aspect of low-cost cookery is to make sure that you and your family eat well and wisely. There is no gain in saving money if it means that your health and well-being are going to suffer. So any attempts to cut the food budget must not jeopardize the main reason for eating food. We must always provide our bodies with everything that they require to function as efficiently as possible and give us the energy we need.

Good nutrition is at the core of cooking on a budget. All the recipes have been devised with healthy eating in mind, so that they help to provide the body with the nutrients that are needed.

Luckily, economical meals don't have to be boring. Tasty, imaginative food can be very inexpensive. You can make the most marvellous meals with fresh, seasonal vegetables and fruit, cheaper cuts of meat and poultry and less expensive types of fish. If you shop wisely you can save lots of money, but first it's a good idea to assess your shopping habits.

Shop wisely

Think about the way you shop and decide if there may be a more sensible approach that could save you money. If you're cooking for others, you'll have to consider their likes and dislikes, and the family's eating patterns. These days many people eat at different times of the day, instead of dining together, and this affects the type of food that is bought.

Next time you go to the supermarket, look at the way other people shop and spend. Those who load their trolleys with convenience foods, ready-meals and snacks will be spending far more than others who purchase simple, unprocessed foods. So take a lesson from that and, where possible, stick to the basics. You will find that you'll spend much more money if are buying lots of gimmicky snack foods and fillers, so try to resist the temptation, even if you think it's going to save you time.

Shopping tips

Before you go shopping, write a list. Check the cupboards to make sure that you are not duplicating items that you already have.

If you are feeling really organized, plan the meals for yourself and family for the week to come and shop for those foods. You can buy any extras, such as fresh bread, during the week.

Always do the shopping alone if you can, and stick to your shopping list. Shopping with others often means that lots of unnecessary and expensive impulse buys end up in your trolley – especially if there are children with you!

On certain days of the week, supermarkets cut the price of some of their lines, often just before closing time or at the weekend. Time your shopping to take advantage of these bargains.

Make the most of products that are reduced because they are close to their sell-by dates. But don't buy foods that you don't need just for the sake of a bargain, and be sure to use them quickly.

Supermarket own-brands are usually cheaper than branded goods, and some stores have a range of basic foods that are plainly packed and especially good value.

Save money-off vouchers and coupons, but only for items that you really want. There's no value in spending money on things that you don't need.

You could always use a hand-basket instead of a trolley in the supermarket – it's one way of restricting your purchases!

Sometimes it's wise to shop locally, where you won't be tempted by the vast array of products on sale in much larger stores.

Get to know your local butcher or fishmonger and tell them that you are always on the lookout for a bargain. There's no shame in being a thrifty shopper, so don't be embarrassed about buying mince (ground meat) when the customer next to you is buying fillet steak!

Consider buying certain items in bulk – it could work out much cheaper. But avoid falling into the trap of buying foods in bulk and then end up eating them almost immediately. Sometimes food disappears far too quickly if you have plenty of it.

Choose cheaper foods

Get to know which foods will really save you money. It may mean choosing some unfamiliar cuts of meat or types of fish, so you might have to brush up on some of your cooking skills, but it will be worth it. Follow the hints and tips here to guide you through some of the ways in which you can choose foods more cheaply.

Choose cheaper cuts of meat. These will need longer, more moist methods of cooking, such as stewing, casseroling or braising, so that the meat becomes tender and delicious, but you'll find that it's well worth the wait.

Shoppers invariably go for the straightforward and familiar, particularly when it comes to meat. If you choose something less popular, it's usually cheaper. Oxtail, shin of beef, brisket, hand of pork and belly pork are all exceptionally good value and very tasty too. Rolled breast of lamb makes a cheap and tasty roast, and neck of lamb is superb in stews. Try offal too; liver, kidney and heart can all be delicious when properly prepared.

Poultry is much cheaper than it used to be, and shops and supermarkets often have offers that are really good value for money. It generally works out much cheaper to buy whole chickens rather than portions, so that you can enjoy the best of the bird, then have the leftovers in a stir-fry or risotto. Make the most of the chicken carcass too, by using it to make stock for soup. If you don't want to make soup immediately, freeze it for later.

BAKING BREAD
If you've never tried baking your own bread, perhaps now is the time to give it a go. It's a very satisfying thing to do – quite therapeutic! And whilst there are usually some very good offers for cheap fresh bread in the supermarkets, it's unlikely that they will taste as good as your home-made efforts – what could be fresher than a loaf straight out of the oven.

You can buy all kinds of flours – plain, wholemeal (whole wheat) or mixed grain, for example – to make a variety of interesting breads and rolls. Even speciality breads, such as focaccia, naan breads, etc, which are always the most expensive to buy, are not so difficult to make yourself.

To save on time and fuel, bake a few loaves at once and freeze what you don't need. When they're defrosted, they'll taste as fresh as ever.

SAVING FUEL

There's not much point in saving lots of money on food if you're going to waste it on fuel. Take account of some of these money saving tips:

Always cover saucepans to keep in the heat. A heavy cast-iron casserole dish is a good investment, as are some of the heavy-gauge stainless steel ones. They retain heat well, so you can cook over a low heat.

Cooking food in a microwave oven is very cost effective as the food is cooked quickly and efficiently, using very little electricity. An added bonus is that there is generally less washing-up to do, so you use less hot water.

Make full use of oven space whenever possible. There's not much point in cooking just a couple of baked potatoes when you could make full use of the oven. Plan what dishes you are going to cook, making sure that they will use the same oven temperature.

Avoid opening the oven door when you are cooking. Not only will you be risking the success of your baking, you will be increasing fuel costs.

Cook more than one vegetable at a time by using a steamer stacked on top of a saucepan. This conserves both fuel and the nutritive value of the vegetables.

If you cook by gas, make sure that the flames stay beneath the saucepan. If they are leaping up the sides of the pan you are wasting fuel.

Even minced (ground) beef can be pretty highly-priced these days, so make a little go a long way by padding it out with extra vegetables. For instance, if you're making a chilli con carne, you can use less mince (ground meat) and add more onions, carrots, mushrooms and red kidney beans to the cooking pot. You won't affect the end result – it will be every bit as tasty, yet considerably cheaper.

Greengrocer's market stalls can be the best place to buy your fruit and vegetables. You can usually get a far better price per pound than anywhere else, and there are often reductions at the end of the day.

Use fruit and vegetables when they are fresh. That way they will have a higher vitamin content, and they will taste better too. So don't buy too many goods at once, or else your produce will deteriorate before you get the chance to eat it.

Start to use the parts of vegetables that you used to throw away. The outer leaves or tougher stalks can all be cooked to make very tasty soups. Once they are chopped finely or puréed, they will taste superb.

If you cut the crusts off sliced bread, make them into breadcrumbs for using in puddings, stuffings and breadcrumb toppings. Or use them to coat chicken pieces or fish. If you don't want to use the breadcrumbs right away, dry them out in a low oven and keep them in an airtight container to use another time.

Canned beans and pulses are great for convenience, but it's much cheaper to soak your own and slow-cook them until tender. Do plenty in one go, then freeze any that you don't use immediately. Remember, however, that it's important to bring dried red kidney beans to the boil and boil rapidly for 10 minutes, to destroy a harmful toxin in them.

You can easily sprout your own beans for salads and stir-fries – mung beans are usually used. All you need do is wash them, then leave them on paper towels and keep them well watered until they sprout – this will take 4–5 days. Rinse well before using.

Freezing foods

A freezer is a good investment for those on a budget. Don't buy one that's larger than you really need, however, as empty freezer space costs money. A full freezer is more efficient, so keep it well stocked up – bread is always a good filler if your stocks are running low.

A freezer means you can buy seasonal produce when it is at its cheapest, make the most of special offers at your supermarket, or freeze any leftovers. If a dish is suitable for freezing, such as a casserole or bake, double the quantities and freeze half – you'll save on fuel and have a ready-made meal just waiting to be reheated whenever you need it. For safety's sake, when reheating frozen foods make sure you heat them thoroughly, to kill any harmful bacteria that may be present.

Get growing

There are so many books available now on growing your own fruit and vegetables, you may as well have a go at producing your own. Even if you only grow a couple of varieties, you may be able to swap some of them with someone else's home-grown produce to get a good selection. And how good they will taste, freshly picked from your own garden.

If you don't have a big enough garden to grow your own fruit and vegetables, don't give up entirely. You can always grow fresh herbs in a few planters and window boxes. They will make a world of difference to your cooking, and will thrive if you keep cutting and using them.

One grow-bag can be used to plant about three tomato plants – enough to keep you in fresh tomatoes throughout the summer, and give you some for chutney-making too. Green or red (bell) peppers will do well too, as will courgettes (zucchini) or cucumbers.

Try buying plants or seeds from local gardening clubs or allotment associations, where they are likely to be much cheaper than garden centres, or swap cuttings with friends and neighbours. You might pick up some friendly advice too.

When it comes to cooking fresh vegetables (whether or not you've grown them yourself) always cook them in a small amount of water for the minimum amount of time. Vegetables should retain their crispness and colour – overcooking them only spoils their flavour and reduces their vitamin content.

Food for free

At certain times of the year, you can take advantage of nature's harvest and help yourself to some free food! Blackberries are to be enjoyed in September, and they are superb in pies and for making jam. Combine them with some apples – the tart flavour complements them perfectly.

Orchards often have an abundant supply of windfalls that you may be allowed to gather. It's a great way to enjoy apples, pears and plums. Or go gathering nuts if you happen to have nut trees near you.

Accept free food from friends graciously. They may not want to make a batch of raspberry jam from their home-grown produce, yet would be glad to see them used by you. The same goes for green tomatoes at the end of the season, which make delicious chutney.

Keep on cooking

Whatever your reasons are for cooking on a budget, it's very wise to treat food as a precious commodity that deserves careful preparation and treatment. After all, a great deal of time and effort goes into its production. And because waste is so unnecessary and expensive, it makes good sense to eat sensibly and healthily. So do make every effort to enjoy good, honest home-cooked food that doesn't cost a fortune: you'll be doing yourself, and your pocket, a great big favour.

LEFTOVERS

Don't be tempted to throw away even the smallest amounts of foods or leftovers. It's surprising how they can easily be used to make something tasty.

Leftover vegetables can be used to flavour stocks, soups and stews, or used for omelette fillings or hashes. You can even mash them and form them into little patties, then coat in beaten egg and breadcrumbs and fry in a little oil.

For your health's sake, treat leftovers with respect – you don't want to end up with a tummy upset. Always cover and cool cooked leftovers quickly, then refrigerate them. Use them up as soon as possible, and reheat thoroughly where appropriate.

INDEX

Apples, pancakes with butterscotch sauce and, 68
apricot and banana queen of puddings, 70
aubergines (eggplant): minced (ground) lamb and potato moussaka, 29

Bacon, onion and potato hotpot, 32
baking, 76–7
bananas: apricot and banana queen of puddings, 70
barley: lamb and barley broth, 12
batter: savoury batter puddings with thyme and onion sauce, 30
beans, 78
beef: baked stuffed onions, 22
beef goulash, 18
bread, 77, 78
chocolate bread pudding, 64
savoury bread and butter pudding, 52
butterscotch sauce, pancakes with apples and, 68

Cakes, 76
cheese: cream cheese and fresh herb soup, 8
golden cheese and leek potato cakes, 58
minced (ground) lamb and potato moussaka, 29
mushroom and Parmesan risotto, 38
pasta with pine nuts (kernels) and blue cheese, 41
savoury bread and butter pudding, 52
spinach and cheese pancake stack, 55
winter vegetable cobbler, 24
chick-peas (garbanzo beans): egg and chick-pea (garbanzo bean) curry, 50
chicken: chicken and chilli bean pot, 16
chicken and sweetcorn puff, 56
quick Chinese chicken with noodles, 44
Thai-style chicken fried rice, 36
chilli: chicken and chilli bean pot, 16
chocolate bread pudding, 64
choux pastry: chicken and sweetcorn puff, 56
cobbler, winter vegetable, 24
coffee cream trifle, 74
coley: mariner's pie, 26
couscous, Moroccan vegetable, 46
cream cheese and fresh herb soup, 8
cucumber dip, 50
curry, egg and chick-pea (garbanzo bean), 50

Desserts, 63–74

dip, cucumber, 50

Eggplant see aubergines
eggs: egg and chick-pea (garbanzo bean) curry, 50
flamenco eggs, 60

Fish stew, Italian, 15
flamenco eggs, 60
free food, 79
freezing foods, 78
fruit, 78
fudge sauce, hot, 64
fuel: saving fuel, 78

Garbanzo beans see chick-peas
golden cheese and leek potato cakes, 58
goulash, beef, 18
growing vegetables, 78–9

Herbs: cream cheese and fresh herb soup, 8
hotpot: bacon, onion and potato, 32

Italian fish stew, 15

Lamb: lamb and barley broth, 12
minced (ground) lamb and potato moussaka, 29
lasagne, smoked fish, 42
leeks: golden cheese and leek potato cakes, 58
mariner's pie, 26
leftovers, 79
lentil and parsnip pottage, 10

Mariner's pie, 26
meat, 77–8
meringue: apricot and banana queen of puddings, 70
minced (ground) lamb and potato moussaka, 29
Moroccan vegetable couscous, 46
moussaka, minced (ground) lamb and potato, 29
mushroom and Parmesan risotto, 38

Noodles, quick Chinese chicken with, 44

Onions: bacon, onion and potato hotpot, 32
baked stuffed onions, 22
savoury batter puddings with thyme and onion sauce, 30
ovens, 78

Pancakes: pancakes with apples and butterscotch sauce, 68

spinach and cheese pancake stack, 55
paprika: beef goulash, 18
parsnips: lentil and parsnip pottage, 10
pasta: pasta with pine nuts (kernels) and blue cheese, 41
smoked fish lasagne, 42
pastry, 76
pearl barley: lamb and barley broth, 12
peppers: beef goulash, 18
pine nuts (kernels), pasta with blue cheese and, 41
plums: baked semolina pudding with spiced plums, 73
pork: savoury batter puddings with thyme and onion sauce, 30
potatoes: bacon, onion and potato hotpot, 32
flamenco eggs, 60
golden cheese and leek potato cakes, 58
mariner's pie, 26
minced (ground) lamb and potato moussaka, 29

Queen of puddings, apricot and banana, 70
quick Chinese chicken with noodles, 44
quick syrup sponge, 66

Red kidney beans: chicken and chilli bean pot, 16
rice: mushroom and Parmesan risotto, 38
Thai-style chicken fried rice, 36
risotto, mushroom and Parmesan, 38

Sauce, hot fudge, 64
saving fuel, 78
savoury bread and butter pudding, 52
savoury batter puddings with thyme and onion sauce, 30
semolina pudding with spiced plums, 73
shopping, 76–7
smoked fish lasagne, 42
soups, 7–12
cream cheese and fresh herb soup, 8
lamb and barley broth, 12
lentil and parsnip pottage, 10
spinach and cheese pancake stack, 55
steaming, 78
stews: beef goulash, 18
chicken and chilli bean pot, 16
Italian fish stew, 15
sweetcorn: chicken and sweetcorn puff, 56
syrup sponge, quick, 66

Thai fish sauce, 36

Thai red curry paste, 36
Thai-style chicken fried rice, 36
tomatoes: beef goulash, 18
chicken and chilli bean pot, 16
minced (ground) lamb and potato moussaka, 29
trifle, coffee cream, 74

Vegetables, 78
Moroccan vegetable couscous, 46
winter vegetable cobbler, 24

Winter vegetable cobbler, 24

Yogurt: cucumber dip, 50